DATE DUE

Inside My Body

What Happens To Broken Bones?

Carol Ballard

Raintree

Chicago, Illinois

www.heinemannraintree.com
Visit our website to find out
more information about
Heinemann-Raintree books.

To order:
☎ Phone 888-454-2279
🖳 Visit www.heinemannraintree.com
   to browse our catalog and order online.

Edited by Kate de Villiers and Vaarunika Dharmapala
Designed by Steve Mead
Illustrations by KJA-artists.com
Picture research by Mica Brancic

Originated by Capstone Global Library Ltd
Printed in the United States of America by Worzalla
Publishing

15 14 13 12 11 10
10 9 8 7 6 5 4 3 2 1

Library of Congress Cataloging-in-Publication Data
Ballard, Carol.
    What happens to broken bones? : bones / Carol Ballard.
       p. cm. — (Inside my body)
    Includes bibliographical references and index.
    ISBN 978-1-4109-4011-7 (hc) — ISBN 978-1-4109-
    4022-3 (pb) 1. Fractures—Juvenile literature. 2. Bones—
    Wounds and injuries—Juvenile literature. 3. Bones—
    Juvenile literature. I. Title. II. Title: Bones.
    RD101.B265 2011
    617.1'5—dc22
                                    2010024673

Acknowledgments
The author and publisher are grateful to the following
for permission to reproduce copyright material: Corbis
pp. **4** (© Tom Stewart), **22** (© Ed Bock), **27** (Jose L.
Pelaez/© JLP); Getty Images pp. **8** (Visuals Unlimited/
Dr. Kessel & Dr. Kardon/Tissues & Organs), **14**
(Photographer's Choice/Tanya Constantine), **16** (The
Image Bank/Dana Menussi), **18** (Photodisc/Noah Clayton),
21 bottom (Photodisc/Steve Mason), **23** (Stone/Dorothy
Riess MD), **25** (Photographer's Choice/Joe McBride), **26**
(Photodisc/Compassionate Eye Foundation/Christa Renee);
iStockphoto.com p. **5** (© Richard Gerstner); Science Photo
Library pp. **10** (Steve Gschmeissner), **13**, **17** (Biophoto
Associates), **21 top** (Dept of Clinical Radiology, Salisbury
District Hospital); Shutterstock pp. **25 band aid** (© Isaac
Marzioli), **25 gauze** (© Yurok).

Cover photograph of a girl with her arm in a cast
reproduced with permission of Shutterstock (Robert O.
Brown Photography).

We would like to thank David Wright for his invaluable
help in the preparation of this book.

Every effort has been made to contact copyright holders
of any material reproduced in this book. Any omissions
will be rectified in subsequent printings if notice is given
to the publisher.

Contents

Words that appear in the text in bold, **like this**, are explained in the glossary on page 30.

What Happens to Broken Bones?

Ouch! Accidents such as falling off a bicycle can break bones. But bones do not stay broken forever. Instead, they slowly heal and get strong again.

A broken bone usually means a trip to the hospital. There, doctors will examine the bone. An X-ray will show them exactly how and where it is broken. Then they can decide what treatment it needs.

Most broken bones need to be kept still. This is so the two broken ends can heal back together. Often a simple **plaster cast** can do this. It is taken off after a few weeks, when the bones have healed. More serious breaks may need metal pins to hold the bones together. These may have to be left in place forever.

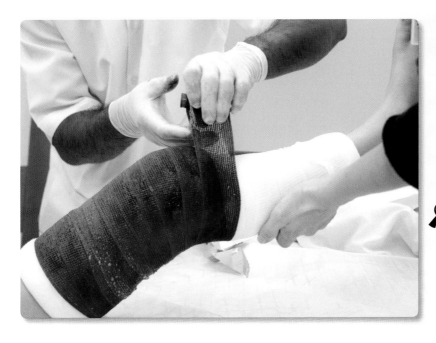

🔍 A doctor is putting a plaster cast on this person's broken leg to keep the bones in place as they heal.

Using crutches

It can be difficult to do everyday things with a broken bone! For example, someone who breaks a leg may need to use crutches to walk for a while. A broken arm may mean someone needs to write and eat with the "wrong" hand for a few weeks.

Sometimes a person who has broken a bone needs to do special exercises. These help rebuild the strength in the bone and the muscles around it.

Why Do I Need Bones?

We all have bones inside our bodies. Have you ever thought about why you need them? What would your body be like if you did not have any bones?

Bones do four important jobs:

1. Support: Your skeleton of bones provides a strong framework. This supports the rest of your body. It also gives your body its shape. Without your bones, you would be like a lump of wobbly jelly!

2. Protect: Some important parts of your body are very fragile. Bones protect them, preventing them from being damaged. For example, your skull bones protect your brain. Your ribs protect your heart and lungs.

3. Allow movement: Your bones cannot move on their own, but they can be pulled into new positions by muscles, which enable you to move.

4. Make blood: The marrow at the center of some bones, such as the pelvis and thighbones, makes **red blood cells**.

How long do bones take to mend and heal?

Every break is different. Small bones mend more quickly than big bones. Simple breaks mend more quickly than complicated breaks. A broken arm usually needs to be in a **plaster cast** for about six weeks. It will take a little longer after that for it to regain full strength.

Extreme body fact

Did you know?
The skeleton of an adult human contains 206 bones.

This diagram shows the bones of a human skeleton. Can you see how the skeleton gives the body its shape?

What Types of Bones Do I Have?

Bones come in all shapes and sizes! The shape and size of a bone depends on the job it has to do. Different bones are good at doing different jobs.

This is an enlarged photograph of the stirrup, the smallest bone in the human body. It is inside the ear. It is 3 to 3.5 millimeters long (about 1/10 of an inch)!

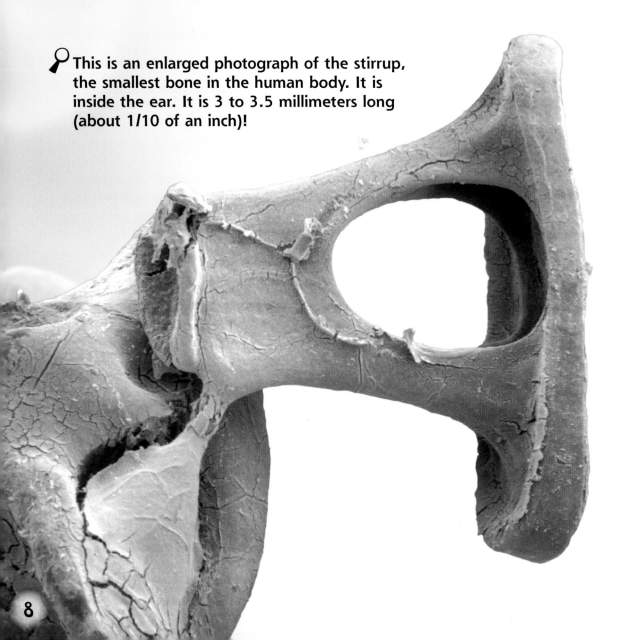

Groups of bones

Bones are sorted into five groups, depending on their shape:

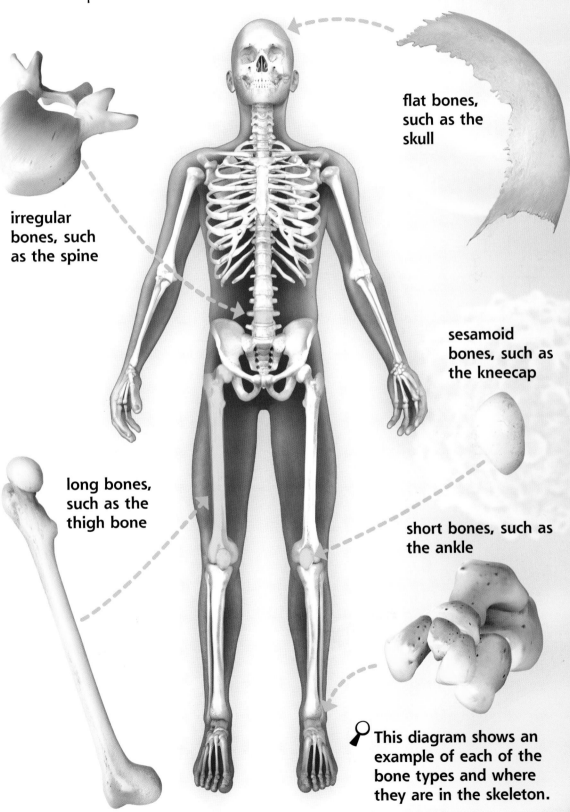

flat bones, such as the skull

irregular bones, such as the spine

sesamoid bones, such as the kneecap

long bones, such as the thigh bone

short bones, such as the ankle

🔍 This diagram shows an example of each of the bone types and where they are in the skeleton.

What Is Inside My Bones?

Bones are made up of several layers. They also contain **blood vessels** and **nerves**.

Inside a bone

All bones are covered by a tough, strong layer. Blood vessels and nerves run through it. Beneath it is a dense, hard material called **compact bone**. This is a network of bony columns. Blood vessels also run through the middle of these.

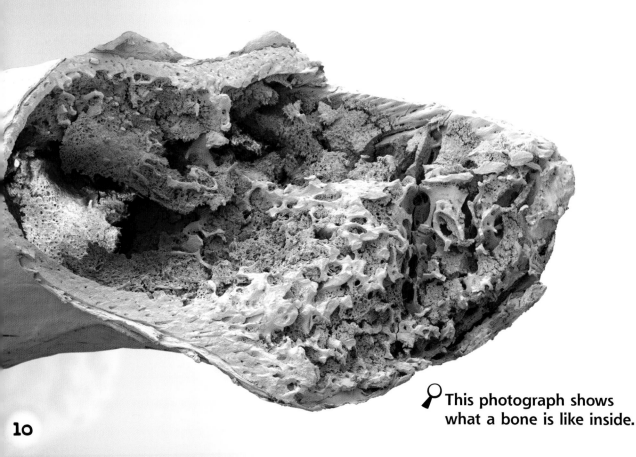

🔍 **This photograph shows what a bone is like inside.**

At the center of the bone is a softer, light material called **spongy bone**. This forms a mesh. In many bones, the spaces in the mesh are filled with bone marrow. This is a little like a jelly. There are two types of bone marrow:

- Red bone marrow in the ribcage, hip bones, and at the ends of long bones makes new **red blood cells**.
- Yellow bone marrow in the long bones is fatty.

Strong bones

Bones contain minerals. The most important mineral is **calcium**. If you eat a healthy diet, your bones will contain about twice as much calcium when you are 15 years old as when you were 10 years old. The extra calcium makes your bones thicker and stronger as you grow up.

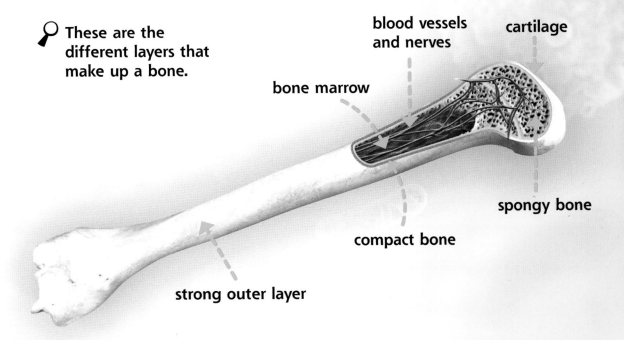

These are the different layers that make up a bone.

blood vessels and nerves

cartilage

bone marrow

spongy bone

compact bone

strong outer layer

What Is a Joint?

The place where two or more bones meet is called a **joint**. Without joints, your skeleton would be rigid and you would not be able to move.

Types of joint

Different types of joint allow different types of movement:

- Hinge joints: These allow movement in one direction, such as back and forth or up and down. Your elbow is a hinge joint.

- Ball and socket joints: These allow movement in almost every direction. Your shoulder and hip joints are ball and socket joints.

SCIENCE BEHIND THE MYTH

MYTH: Being double-jointed means you have two joints instead of one.

SCIENCE: No, it does not! It just means that one or some of your joints are more flexible than most people's. For example, you might be able to bend your thumb or your elbow backward, or you might have a very flexible back.

- Fixed joints: These do not allow any movement. The joints between the bones in your skull are fixed joints.

- Gliding joints: These let bones glide smoothly over each other. There are gliding joints in your wrists and ankles.

- Pivot joints: These let one bone swivel around on top of another. The pivot joint at the top of your neck lets you turn your head from side to side.

Most joints occur where the ends of two bones meet. They are held together by strong fibers called **ligaments**. Fluid between the bones allows them to move easily and stops them from rubbing on each other.

In this X-ray you can see how the balls (circled) at the top of the thigh bones fit snugly into the sockets in the pelvis.

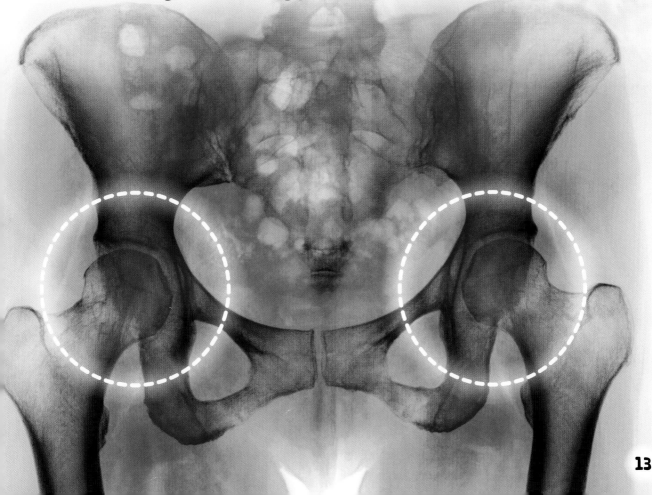

How Do I Move?

Bones cannot move themselves. Instead, muscles pull them into new positions.

Most of your muscles are attached to bones by strong bands called **tendons**. Some muscles are attached by a single tendon at each end. Others are attached by many tendons.

Each muscle can contract, which means it makes itself shorter. Muscles work in pairs to move bones.

The muscle at the front of your upper arm bulges when you bend your arm.

Bend your arm

You can see how muscles contract if you move your lower arm:

- Hold one arm out straight in front of you. Put your other hand on top of the upper half of your arm.
- Now bend your arm. Can you feel the muscle bulge under your hand? It has contracted to pull the bones up. This stretches the muscle at the back of your arm.
- Now straighten your arm. You should feel the bulge vanish. This is because the muscle is stretched as the muscle at the back of your arm contracts to pull the bones down.

Practical advice

Twists, sprains, and strains

If you twist or strain any of the muscles in a **joint**, it may swell. Try RICE to relieve pain and swelling:

1. **R**est—to prevent more damage
2. **I**ce—place an ice pack on the joint
3. **C**ompression—wrap a bandage around the joint
4. **E**levation—keep the joint raised.

How Do Bones Grow?

You are much bigger now than when you were born. But do you know how your bones actually grow?

Cartilage

🔍 Measure your height every few months to see how fast you are growing!

Babies are born with more than 300 bones. Their bones contain a soft, flexible material called **cartilage**. As the baby grows, the cartilage becomes hard and turns into bone. Some of the bones join together to make the 206 bones of an adult skeleton.

Long bones, such as those in your arms and legs, grow from special growth plates found at each end. These make new cartilage, leaving the older cartilage near the middle of the bone. This old cartilage then turns into bone. When the bone has finished growing, the growth plates also turn into bone.

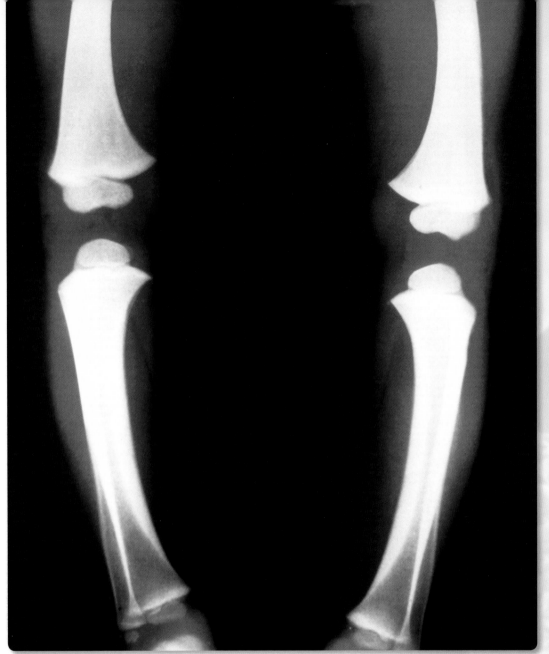

🔍 This X-ray shows the bent leg bones of a child suffering from rickets.

When bones do not grow correctly

Sometimes bones do not grow as they should. If children do not have enough vitamin D or **calcium** in their bodies, they can get a condition called rickets. This can cause pain, weak muscles, bent legs, and slowed growth. Luckily, rickets can be treated and cured.

How Do Bones Break?

Bones are strong enough to stand up to most ordinary activities, but a very strong force or an awkward bend can snap them.

A broken bone is usually the result of an accident, such as falling off a bicycle or out of a tree. Bones can break in different ways. Some breaks are more serious and take longer to heal than others.

🔍 Oh no! A fall from a tree could result in a broken bone.

Types of break

This table shows some different types of break:

type of break	what happens to the bone
simple	the bone breaks into two, but the pieces stay in their correct places
compound	the bone breaks into two, and one or both pieces stick out through the skin
greenstick	one side of a young child's bone breaks, but the other side just bends
comminuted	the bone breaks into two, and some of it shatters into tiny pieces
impacted	the bone breaks into two, and one piece is pushed into the other

Fragile bones

Most people have very few broken bones during their lifetime. However, some children are born with an illness called brittle bone disease. Their bones can break very easily. A condition called osteoporosis can also make bones more fragile and likely to break. Osteoporosis is most common in elderly people, especially women.

SCIENCE BEHIND THE MYTH

MYTH: Sunshine makes your bones strong.

SCIENCE: It's true! Sunshine does help to keep bones strong and healthy. Your body makes vitamin D using the ultraviolet (UV) rays in sunlight. Vitamin D is needed to help your body absorb **calcium** from your food. Without calcium, bones are weak.

How Do I Know if It Is Broken?

Sometimes it is obvious that a bone has broken after an accident. At other times, it can be less easy to tell.

So, what are the signs that a bone may be broken? Here are some questions you can ask yourself if you are not sure:

- Did you hear a crack or a snap during the accident?
- Is the area around the injury swollen or bruised?
- Does it hurt to put weight on the injury, or to touch it or move it?

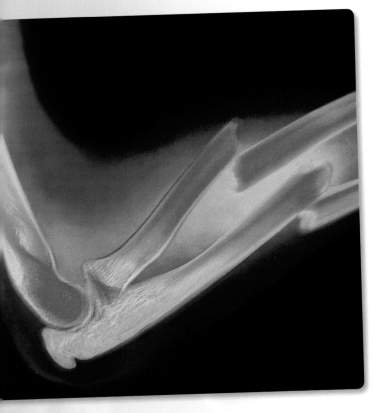

- Is the injured part shaped strangely?
- Can you see bone poking through the skin?

🔍 **In this X-ray you can see how the bones of a lower arm have snapped.**

If the answer is "yes" to most of these, there is a good chance the bone is broken. It can be a big shock to break a bone, and people often feel dizzy, sick, and upset for a while. However, they soon get over the shock and start to feel better.

Remember, too, that an injury can hurt an awful lot even if no bones are broken!

Paramedics will use this stretcher to carry the injured skier. They will keep her as still as possible after her fall. At the hospital, an X-ray will tell doctors if any bones are broken.

How Do Bones Mend?

Luckily, a bone does not stay broken forever. Bones can heal and mend themselves.

Most broken bones require a trip to the hospital. An X-ray will show doctors exactly where the bone is broken and what type of break it is.

If it is a simple break, a **plaster cast** or **fiberglass cast** may be the only treatment needed. This holds the pieces of bone in place while they heal.

🔍 **Plaster casts come in many colors. It can be fun to get your friends to sign your cast!**

A slow process

Complicated breaks may require an operation. Sometimes steel pins or screws are inserted. These add strength around the break and keep the ends of the bones in place.

The bone will slowly begin to heal. **Blood vessels** grow into the area around the break. A few days after this, a substance called **collagen** forms around the break. Slowly this turns into tough **cartilage**, which forms a bridge between the pieces of bone. A hard, bony shell forms. It is slowly replaced with hard **compact bone**. Eventually, the bone is fully healed.

🔍 **Metal pins like these ones may be removed when the bones have healed, but sometimes they have to stay in place forever.**

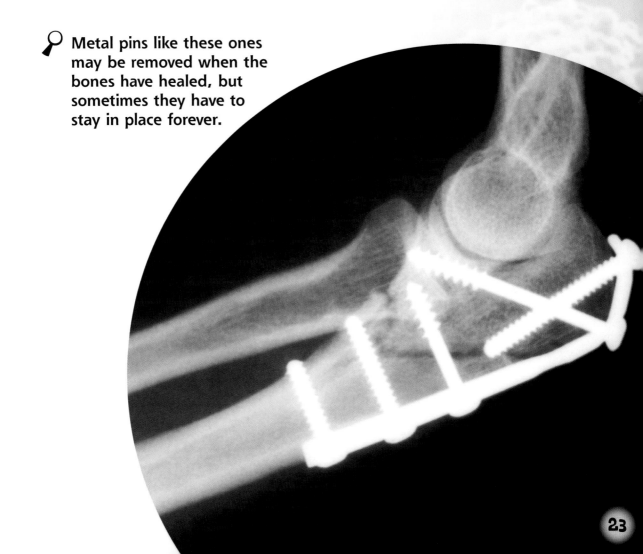

How Can I Take Care of My Bones?

Your bones are important. They need to last your whole life, so it makes sense to keep them strong and healthy. Follow these tips to help you do this.

Food for bones

Calcium helps to give bones their strength. Your body gets this from the food you eat. Try to eat foods that are rich in calcium, such as oily fish, eggs, milk, and milk products such as cheese, butter, and yogurt.

Exercise and bones

Regular, hard exercise can help your bones to stay strong. Scientists have proved this by studying astronauts. When astronauts are weightless in space, moving is much easier because there is no gravity to work against. They slowly lose bone mass because they do not have to work hard enough. Try to do activities that make your body work hard. Gymnastics, dancing, running, and playing basketball are all good for your bones as well as your muscles.

Protecting bones

Try to avoid broken bones by wearing the correct protective clothing for your activity. This includes things such as:

- bicycle helmets
- elbow pads, knee pads, and helmets for skateboarding
- body shields and hard hats for horse riding.

Practical advice

After a broken bone

When a bone has healed, your doctor will remove the cast. Your bone will still be weak, so you cannot start playing sports or doing other activities right away. Your doctor may suggest exercises to help your bone and muscles become strong again.

This boy's helmet, elbow pads, and knee pads will protect some of his bones as he skateboards.

All About Bones

Think of some of the things you did today. Did you get out of bed, brush your teeth, and run downstairs? Did you walk or cycle to school? Did you throw a ball or do a cartwheel? You could not have done any of these things without your skeleton!

🔍 **Being active can help your bones to grow strong!**

Stronger than concrete

Bones come in all sorts of shapes and sizes, depending on the job each bone has to do. Together, all your bones make up about 10 to 15 percent of your total weight. Bones are very strong. If you compared a bone with the same weight of concrete, you would find the bone is stronger!

With help from your doctor, your broken bone will mend itself.

You cannot see them, and may not even think about them very often, but your bones are really important. Treat them well, and they will grow strong and last you a lifetime!

Amazing Skeleton Facts

Collarbones are one of the most commonly broken bones. They are the bones that run from your neck across the front of your shoulder.

The longest, strongest, and heaviest bone is the thigh bone. In adults, the thigh bone is usually about one-quarter of the person's height.

The tallest person ever to be measured was Robert Pershing Wadlow. He was 2.72 meters (8 feet, 11 inches) tall! If he stretched his arms out, his fingertips were more than 2.88 meters (9 feet, 6 inches) apart.

Did you know that you are taller in the morning than you are in the evening? The bones of your spine press down on each other during the day. They squeeze the discs of **cartilage** that lie between them. When you lie down, the discs slowly return to their full size.

The world record for having broken the most bones is held by a motorcycle stunt rider named Evel Knievel. He broke at least 35 bones in his body!

The main bones in your body

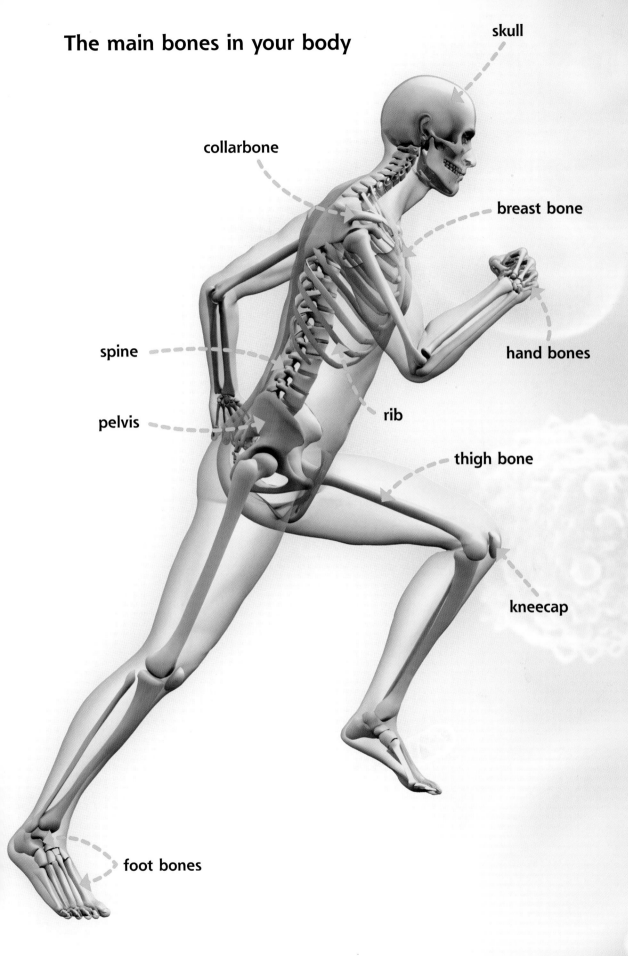

skull

collarbone

breast bone

hand bones

spine

pelvis

rib

thigh bone

kneecap

foot bones

Glossary

blood vessel tube through which blood travels around the body

calcium mineral that the body needs to keep bones and teeth strong and healthy

cartilage type of strong, flexible material that cushions and protects bones

collagen material formed as a broken bone heals

compact bone dense, hard material below the outer layer of a bone

fiberglass cast strong, light material put around a broken bone to hold it still while it heals

joint place where the ends of two or more bones meet

ligament strong, stretchy tissue that holds joints together

nerve part of the body that carries signals to and from the brain

plaster cast strong, hard casing put around a broken bone to hold it still while it heals

red blood cell part of the blood that carries oxygen around the body

spongy bone soft, light material at the center of a bone

tendon strong, rope-like part that joins muscles to bones

Find Out More

Books

Bailey, Jacqui. *What Happens When You Move?* (*How Your Body Works*). New York: PowerKids, 2009.

Green, Jen. *Skeleton* (*Your Body and Health*). Mankato, Minn.: Stargazer, 2006.

Spilsbury, Louise. *The Skeleton and Muscles* (*The Human Machine*). Chicago: Heinemann Library, 2008.

Websites

http://kidshealth.org/kid/htbw/bones.html

Learn more about bones at this website for kids.

http://kidshealth.org/parent/general/aches/cast_faq. html

This website answers frequently asked questions about getting a cast.

http://depts.washington.edu/bonebio/

This website has lots of information about bones, including how to build bone strength and details about bone diseases.

Index